One of the most perc[...] [...]
ever read, *Prone to* [...]
conflicts of the Christian life. But Natalie Brand does
more. She comes along side us, pointing out that we are
not alone in the battle and that there is a 'way of escape'
giving us hope and renewed confidence in the power of
the cross.

FAITH COOK
Author of several books, including *Troubled Journey* and *Sound
of Trumpets*

Natalie's gospel-filled warnings mix clarity with compassion.
I hope many will be kept from shipwreck by the earthy
wisdom of this book.

JOEL VIRGO
Senior Pastor, Emmanuel Church, Brighton

Our sinful hearts incline us to turn away from the Lord,
and we find ourselves spiritually in the wastelands. This
little book is a winsome word to believers who struggle
or stray, to return to Christ the friend of sinners. Help
is given in diagnosing our spiritual need, pointing us to
Christ, and taking practical steps for a more constant walk
with the Lord. Warmly commended!

BILL JAMES
Principal of London Seminary

The drum-beat of *Prone to Wander* is: God pursues His
children. Natalie makes it clear that backsliding is the
result of sin, but lifts God up as compassionate to sinners.
She uses helpful biblical and contemporary illustrations

to explain why we slide and gives gospel comfort and practical tips to end the descent. Are you running from God like Jonah? Are you weighed down with sorrow and suffering like Job? Are you, like David, desperate because of your own sin? Pick up this book and find help for your soul.

KERI FOLMAR
Pastor's wife, United Christian Church of Dubai, and author of *The Good Portion: Scripture*

Natalie writes as a friend talking to a friend, balancing personal honesty and sympathy with the wisdom and challenge of Biblical truth. This book did my soul good. As one who is 'prone to wander' it engaged my mind, warmed my heart, and redirected my steps towards the God I love.

JANE MCNABB
Conference speaker and Chair of London Women's Convention

Pastors and counselors who routinely seek to restore wandering Christians would do well to keep copies of this book as handy as a box of Kleenex. Christians seeking to restore a wandering brother or sister should get and give this book to their friend as quickly as they'd perform the Heimlich on a choking diner. And the rest of us? Well, I can't speak for you, but, now that I think about it, *Prone to Wander* is a pretty good description of me...

C. L. CHASE
Author of *Grace-Focused Optimism*

We are all prone to wander, but what does that mean for the life of faith? In this wonderful work, Natalie Brand carefully explores the Christian's tendency toward unbelief and spiritual distraction. Drawing from scripture, she offers a perspective on how we should respond to such a tendency, and she does it in a way that is biblical, practical, and sensitive to actual human experience.

SCOTT REDD
President and Associate Professor of Old Testament,
Washington, D.C. campus of Reformed Theological Seminary

NATALIE BRAND

PRONE TO
WANDER

GRACE FOR THE LUKEWARM
AND APATHETIC

CHRISTIAN
FOCUS

Copyright © Natalie Brand 2018

paperback ISBN 978-1-5271-0208-8
epub ISBN 978-1-5271-0247-7
mobi ISBN 978-1-5271-0248-4

First published in 2018
by
Christian Focus Publications Ltd,
Geanies House, Fearn, Ross-shire,
IV20 1TW, Scotland
www.christianfocus.com

A CIP catalogue record for this book is available from the British Library.

Cover design by Paul Lewis

Printed and bound by
Bell & Bain, Glasgow.

Contents

For my Bundle — Hope in a dark place.

Acknowledgements

Special thanks to the Rev. Dr D. Eryl Davies (Dr D) for offering pastoral and theological guidance. Your comments are always so full of wisdom. Also to the gorgeous Sarah Allen for her hard work on the manuscript and encouragement — I wish I had your command of the English language.

Thanks to Angela Brand for her proofreading, and also to my dear friends Rhona Black and Lorna Bradley for helpfully sharing their thoughts. My gratitude and love also to Ken and Beryl Gaines for so willingly babysitting at the last minute. And many thanks to the truly talented Jenny Bright for her beautiful and unique illustrations, and to Rosanna Burton at Christian Focus for faithfully working this project through to completion.

I am indebted to Thomas most of all: for your endless support, personal sacrifices and trawling through my manuscript multiple times. I love that Nicholas is right; you can't put a cigarette paper between us theologically. Thank you also to Georgiana, Beatrice and Arabella who put up with Mummy going off to the hotel to write, and welcomed me back with excited screams and kisses.

Preface

We owe a debt of gratitude to Natalie Brand for tackling an urgent pastoral issue that threatens not only the well-being of God's people individually but the progress of His gospel at a challenging time — our propensity to wander away from the Lord Jesus, our good and kind shepherd. How welcome is the restoration of 'grace' into our thinking and into our vocabulary. Less welcome is the mistaken loss of spiritual responsibility that has sometimes accompanied it. As Natalie helpfully reminds us, grace doesn't mean that sin doesn't matter. Far from it.

With delightful directness and a ruthless willingness to be both deeply personal and painfully honest, Natalie stops us in our tracks through a series of short chapters. Employing the profiles of some of the Bible's biggest names, she charts the reasons for our willingness to wander, offers us helpful remedies when we find ourselves far from the Lord we love and finally makes some practical suggestions that will help us curb our wander-lust. Unsurprisingly, we discover that all we need is the gospel. But if the Lord

Jesus' heart is to give himself to us, our responsibility is to grab him and never let go.

Richard Underwood
Retired Pastoral Ministries Director of FIEC
April 2018

Introduction: Prone to Wander

I can't pray! My tongue feels spiritually tied and guilt churns in my stomach as I glimpse my dust-ridden Bible, untouched for weeks. I find no strength in my arm to lift it; I have no desire, yet feel some longing and mourning for the things of God. I am in a land as dry as Ezekiel's valley; the parched earth is as cracked as my lips. I know I should turn around and trudge back up to the cool mountain springs. But I am robbed of muscle and passion. I am just a wandering pile of dry, lifeless bones.

Yet I am hunted ... hunted by the grace that saved me.

Straying from God

As Christians, many of us experience times when we struggle in our faith. Times when we get distracted, like dumb sheep, and stray away from the safety of the fold and our faithful Shepherd. Some of us wander for months or even years, backsliding into unbelief and serious sin. Others of us fall into spiritual apathy where our passion for Christ cools and we can't pray or pick up our Bibles.

Whether we are lukewarm or backsliding, no matter how far we roam away from God, it is a painful and horrible place to be. We grow unnaturally numb to the goodness of God, the gospel loses its punch, and our sin fails to repulse us.

Honest to God

Robert Robinson was a man who was honest about his tendency to drift from the Lord. In his hymn 'Come Thou Fount of Every Blessing', Robinson confesses that he isn't just at risk of straying away from God ... he is susceptible to it.

> *Prone to wander, Lord I feel it.*
> *Prone to leave the God I love.*[1]

Robinson's words have always resonated with me. I too feel this stupid inclination inside me. Not a week goes by when I don't wrestle with a distracted or cold heart towards God. Sure, this is because I am just human. But it is mostly because I am a sinner.

As we shall see, sometimes we are lukewarm because life has knocked us down, and we are dry and burnt out. Other times it is because we are deliberately wandering away: choosing sin. For 'All we like sheep have gone astray; we have turned — *every one* — to his own way' (Isa. 53:6, emphasis added). As believers in Christ we are saved by grace but our sin can still drive us away from our loving God.

---

1. 'Come thou fount of every blessing', Robert Robinson, 1758.

Luke Warm

Meet Mr Luke Warm. After every church service Luke would always stand with his arms crossed, resting against the wall of the church bookshop, looking sharp in his faded jeans and designer sunglasses. About a year or so ago Luke started to leave his Bible at church during the week. 'So I know it's here when I need it,' he would say. Although he helped with the chairs every week and hosted Christianity Explored in his apartment, Luke never prayed publicly anymore. And he talked about sermons in the same way he talked about Michael McIntyre. Luke had just become too cool to burn passionately for Christ … so he carried on spiritually tepid.

In the book of Revelation Christ rebukes the Christians in Laodicea because their faith had turned lukewarm and flat; like a bottle of Coke left out in the sun too long. Although they looked the same on the outside, they had shrivelled up on the inside and lost their fire for Jesus (Rev. 3:14-22). Their problem was their materialism and comfort (v. 17), and this can be our pitfall too.

Life Pressures

Some time ago my love for Christ cooled into a pool of disgusting complacency. I suddenly found it hard to make personal sense of the gospel, and uninvited doubts about the existence of God or whether I was really a Christian would pop into my head. Most of all, my prayer life resembled road-kill.

A host of things contributed to this: as a family we were burnt out in the ministry, dog-tired from broken sleep with our new-born baby and witnessing the end of

17

a family marriage. These were my *triggers* but they were not my *pitfalls*. Such triggers can knock us but they never make us sin. We sin because we choose to. Like the church in Laodicea, my comfort was my stumbling block. Things were hard going and so I looked for the easy ride. I became mentally preoccupied with physical and material ease instead of the comfort given by Jesus Christ.

But grace saved me from my lukewarm Christianity. You've met grace too ... when you first came to Christ.

Rescuing the Backslider

We also wander away from God because we fall into serious sin. This is frequently described as 'backsliding' — a term that suggests a slippery slope and someone sliding down it backwards. Perhaps you are a 'backslidden' Christian. You once were a believer in Christ but now you are in the habit of deliberately choosing sin instead of running from it. Maybe you have even denounced your faith and walked away from the church, or committed adultery, or got stuck into some heavy-duty sin that is crushing you. You know you are lost and you need God to rescue you. Don't be discouraged! God told Ezekiel: 'I *will* seek the lost, and I *will* bring back the strayed' (Ezek. 34:16, emphasis added). Even when we are stuck in a mess of rebellion and unbelief, if we belong to Christ He will rescue us by the grace of His cross.

That Same Grace

So here is hope! The fact you have this book in your hands is a sign that you want out of your apathy and backsliding. Hope lies in the fact that the same grace that first brought you to Christ is available to you now. The grace of the Lord Jesus carries us through the Christian life; it doesn't just dump us at the door and leave the rest to us. Grace is ready for you in Christ … grab it!

Am I a Christian?

'That's all fair enough … But I've been backsliding for a long time now and I don't know whether I was really ever saved.' The point is, whether you are a lukewarm Christian, a backsliding believer, or a wayward prodigal who learnt of God's grace in his younger years but has lived many without it, *we all need the gospel*. In this book we are not going to get caught up in the past and questions of 'when was I saved?' We are going to focus on the gospel and taking hold of Christ now.

This Book

So, whether you would describe yourself as sliding, straying, running, or drifting from God; if you are spiritually cold, lukewarm, dry, thirsty or just plain worn out — whatever the metaphor — this book has been written to give you gospel comfort and practical counsel to help you move Godward.

In three parts, we will explore why as Christians we stray from God, offer comfort in your time of lukewarmness or apathy, and unpack some practical essentials that safeguard us from stumbling in the future. If you are in a place of deep spiritual pain and wrestling then I recommend reading part two first. There are also optional activities to encourage you to take further action and again take hold of King Jesus.

The world is like that tide,
it lulls us away from God

Part One: Why We Stray

There is only one reason we stray from God and it is our sin. Here are five biblical profiles to help us understand why at times we leave the God we love.

1. Running Like Jonah

Jonah's wandering away from God is somewhat legendary … and a little fishy. He didn't just stray from God; he ran. And he ran from God because he was disobeying Him.

As a prophet of God, Jonah was supposed to be one of God's elite. Yet when God sends him off to be a street preacher in what is modern day Iraq, to a people who are Jonah's equivalent of the Islamic State, Jonah hauls off in the other direction (Jonah 1:3). And who can blame him? A holiday in the Mediterranean sounds a lot more appealing.

Lost in a Dark Place

So, this fickle and disobedient prophet runs away 'from the presence of the LORD' (Jonah 1:3). And while Jonah sleeps soundly in his getaway ship, God stirs up a wild storm (vv. 4-6). This stops him in his mutinous tracks, waking him up both physically and spiritually, and he admits to the ship's captain that he is running away from his God, 'the God of heaven, who made the sea' (v. 9). Jonah knows that if he doesn't surrender himself to the waves, he will drag these unbelieving sailors to an early death with him. His disobedience has very quickly turned lethal. But God's grace wastes no time: as the waves envelop him, Jonah is graciously gobbled up by a humongous fish (v. 17).

We sanitise Jonah's story when in reality his backsliding led him to a pretty grim place. It is very probable that Jonah wasn't on his knees praying angelically with only a string of soggy seaweed wrapped around his toes. He spent many long and traumatising hours inside a fish. Jonah describes himself drowning in the 'belly of Sheol' which is a Hebrew term for a place of death (Jonah 2:2). Imagine yourself buried alive inside a flooding coffin; that was Jonah's experience. It would have been pitch black, smelly, and airless. He would have had to fight for breath, especially if he was immersed in water ... hungry, thirsty, exhausted, and fighting his own thoughts to give up and allow himself to drown.

Straying away from God is miserable. Perhaps you know all too well that what starts out as a fun distraction quickly turns ugly and spiritually toxic.

Grace in the Storm

But Jonah was not abandoned ... and neither are you. If you have been backsliding head-first into sin or if you are dry and feel spiritually dead, remember the promise that He '*will* seek the lost' and 'bring back the strayed' (Ezek. 34:16, emphasis added). God's grace is unmistakable in Jonah's story. God's grace was in the storm: He could have just left Jonah to run away. God's grace was in the fish:

He could have left Jonah to drown, but instead sends an unconventional ark to rescue him.

Jesus was your rescuer and ark when you first became a Christian. And He is still your ark today; the safe vessel to bring you out of the lifeless depths and back home to God. You see, even when we run like Jonah, God 'delights in steadfast love' (Micah 7:18). Our Heavenly Father 'will again have compassion on us; he will tread our iniquities underfoot. You will cast all our sins into the depths of the sea' (Micah 7:19).

What Jonah Does

What does Jonah do when the reality of his rebellion against the Lord hits him like a face full of krill? We read in chapter two that Jonah calls out to God for help; he prays. In Jonah's case and in our own, God's grace works together with our responsibility to call upon Him. When we call upon the Lord He listens.

Like Jonah you might be sinking; pulled down in a sea of rebellion. Call out now and God will rescue you. 'The Lord your God is in your midst, a mighty one who will save; he will rejoice over you with gladness; he will quiet you by his love' (Zeph. 3:17).

READ:
So many of Jonah's experiences resemble our own. Carve out 10 minutes now and read the story yourself.

---

2. Drifting to Pleasure Island

Upon moving over to South Wales to study theology, I decided to experience the stunning coastline and enrol in the local surf culture by buying my first surfboard. I found a cheap second-hand board in a shop tucked away in the Mumbles and asked the assistant whether it was suitable for a learner. They said it was, and I purchased it for a mere £70.

I adored that surfboard; I scraped it, waxed it, and lovingly tied it, bagless, to the roof of my VW Polo. And for a few months I lived the Californian dream ... in South Wales. Until it became obvious that the assistant had lied and I was never going to learn to surf on it.

However, I did enjoy paddling out on it into an angry sea and wrestling with the waves; getting 'out-back' beyond the white crashing waves into the deep, dark majesty. That is where you really meet the sea: and boy, you can just lie on your back and revel in the thrill of such a meeting. Of course, you *do* have to keep an eye on the beach. Only a fool would shut their eyes and mindlessly ignore the fact that the tide is mercilessly pulling them from the shore.

Drifting

The world is like that tide; it lulls us away from God. As Christians we backslide in our faith because we lie back, shut our eyes and are happy to be taken. We may experience little naggings here and there — Oh, we missed C.U. or home group again — and we try to ignore them for days or weeks. By the time our alarm finally goes off we have drifted quite a distance from the shore.

Devastating Distraction

Demas was a man who drifted so far from God that he walked out on his friends and ministry. He was one of Paul's most trusted missionary colleagues (*cf.* Col. 4:14, Philem. 1:24). But in his second letter to Timothy, Paul is forced to write: 'Do your best to come to me soon. For Demas, in love with this present world, has deserted me and gone to Thessalonica' (2 Tim. 4:9-10).

We don't know what happened to Demas, but Paul's words are devastating. Demas had deserted God, Paul and his ministry because he had fallen 'in love with this present world'. I think Demas lost heart and started to focus on the 'things seen' instead of 'things that are unseen' (2 Cor. 4:18). Maybe he was seduced by the glamour of the city and had had enough of the hard life on the road as an evangelist — the discouragements, the persecution and the obscurity. Either way, the world seduced Demas and, from what we know, the world won.

Polluted

What's the big problem with the world? Don't we live in the world? Isn't this where God has put us?

Since sin came on the scene in Genesis 3, this world has been polluted. John warns us of this in 1 John 2: 'Do not love the world or the things in the world. If anyone loves the world, the love of the Father is not in him. For all that is in the world — the desires of the flesh and the desires of the eyes and pride of life — is not from the Father but is from the world' (1 John 2:15-16). It is one or the other; we cannot love God and the world.

Return

When we are lukewarm and backsliding it can feel as if God doesn't want us back; as if He is not fighting for us. But His fight was at Calvary and this is where we should look. Whether you are a Christian struggling in the faith, or someone who doubts whether they have ever belonged to Christ, the cross is our only means of returning to God.

The Mend-and-Cleanse Gospel

When I was a teenager, the David Bowie film *Labyrinth* was cult in my circle of friends; we would quote it endlessly to each other. In one scene, the protagonist (a girl trying to rescue her baby brother in a world of changing landscapes and puzzles) nearly falls into a rancid, bubbling swamp called, 'the bog of eternal stench'. One touch and nothing can wash you … you will stink forever.

Not so with the gospel. If we call upon Christ, He will cleanse us from the eternal stench of our sin. The Father's grace in the outstretched, crucified arms of Jesus

Christ are wide enough for everyone; they can cover the murderer, the adulterer, the backslider and the lukewarm. Even if, like Demas, you have fallen headlong in love with the world, wreaked havoc and hurt, and betrayed your family, church, or ministry, in Christ there is no eternal stench. He promises us through His Word: '[My people] shall not defile themselves anymore with their idols and their detestable things, or with any of their transgressions. But I will save them from all the backsliding in which they have sinned, and will cleanse them; and they shall be my people, and I will be their God' (Ezek. 37:23).

THINK: The Slow Bicycle Race

Did you ever ride in a slow bicycle race as a child? I recall very clearly the impossibility of trying to keep on top of your bike whilst trying to go nowhere; awkwardly swinging your front wheel from hard right to hard left to cover as little ground as possible, the twisted handlebars giving you nothing to balance on at all. You just had to make progress or you fell off!

Likewise, there is no such thing as a static Christian life. As believers in Christ we are either pushing forwards into Him or we are falling off; we are either growing up in our faith or we are slipping into a life of godless sin. Have you ever told yourself you are coasting for a bit or 'having a breather', whereas you were actually wandering away from the Lord?

3. The Easy Ride

The Christian life is no punt down the river; Paul the Apostle describes it as a long, hard fight (*cf.* 1 Tim. 6:12, 2 Tim. 4:7). There are times under the strain of this fight when we look for a comfort stop or an easier ride elsewhere. This isn't just harmless spiritual dithering. When we fix our eyes on something other than Christ we are actively choosing a disruptive hiatus. We think we are heading out for a refreshing cruise, relishing a break from rules and responsibilities. But instead the easy ride is frequently a short joy-ride to spiritual self-destruction.

Pitching for the World

Lot, Abraham's nephew, had experienced God's goodness to the extreme. After moving with Abraham (or Abram as he was known then) from his homeland, Lot had tasted God's promises in the land of Canaan and enjoyed great material blessing (Gen. 11:31). God had given Lot so much that he had to part ways with his uncle for the sheer number of their herds and servants. Lot chose to settle in the lush, flat Jordon Valley whilst Abram stayed in the hill country the Lord had set apart (Gen. 13:11-12). Although he was a believer, Lot edged his tent nearer and nearer the evil city of Sodom until he was living within it (Gen. 13:12–14:12 *cf.* 2 Pet. 2:6-8). Like Demas, he literally drifted into the walls of the world; a city of people who were 'wicked, [and] great sinners against the LORD' (Gen. 13:13).

Comfort Seeking

I finally flung myself onto the sofa after a long day of juggling three kids at home, and even more at church. Ignoring the fact it was time to tune into a Sunday evening service online, I killed a couple of hours on eBay, telling myself I needed a break. Actually, I had lost my holy expectancy for God's Word; an absence which had been apparent that morning too, for it normally drove me to church. Instead I went because I didn't want to get into trouble with the pastor (when he came home).

This became normative for weeks. I had slipped into a spiritual lethargy. I was no longer hungry for God's covenant goodness. Instead I was pitching my tent too close to the world. I didn't want God anymore; I wanted the easy ride.

Lingering Lot

While Abram continued to worship the Lord and build altars of thanksgiving, Lot got so mixed up in godless Sodom that Abram had to rescue him from its raiders (Gen. 14:13-16). Then we see God making a history shaking covenant with Abram, changing his name to

Abraham (Gen. 15-17). But Lot is not there. He is back in Sodom, seeking to be at home in a place he was supposed to be only travelling through (Gen. 19:9). In chapter 18 we find God telling Abraham He is going to rain judgment down upon the city. Although Lot stupidly kept returning to Sodom, God graciously pulls him out in time. Yet the crazy thing is, Lot is still reticent to go. The angels of the Lord are literally dragging him away, 'Up! Take your wife and your two daughters who are here, lest you be swept away in the punishment of the city' (Gen. 19:15). What does Lot do? He lingers (Gen. 19:16).

Parched Procrastinator

As a child, my twin sister would frequently get lost half-way down the beach because she was so engrossed in shell collecting. We are like this; so distracted that we heedlessly wander away from God's parental care. Then we decide to return and yet, like Lot, even in this we linger. We linger in our lukewarmness and backsliding instead of turning directly to God in prayer and in his Word. Crawling through the desert parched to death, we beg for a fancy cocktail with a curly straw and a paper umbrella when what we need is water ... pure water!

If you are thirsty for gospel water — dehydrated from your own apathy and sin — your heavenly Father calls to you: 'Come, everyone who thirsts, come to the waters; and he who has no money, come, buy and eat! ... Why do you spend your money for that which is not bread, and your labour for that which does not satisfy?' (Isa. 55:1-2). Do not linger; turn back to Christ now, 'the living water'

(John 4:10) who quenches our spiritual thirst with his own blood at Calvary.

Not Home Yet

When we opt for the easy ride we try to make the Christian faith something it is not; in the words of J. C. Ryle: 'to make the gate more wide, and the cross more light'.[1] In their ease, Demas and Lot settled in cities that were not their home. Yet we need to constantly preach to ourselves that we are not home yet; just as at the end of a holiday, when we can't shake the fact it's coming to an end and we prepare mentally to go home.

READ: Isaiah 55:6-9

Seek the Lord while he may be found;
call upon him while he is near;
let the wicked forsake his way,
and the unrighteous man his thoughts;
let him return to the Lord, that he may have compassion on him,
and to our God, for he will abundantly pardon.
For my thoughts are not your thoughts,
neither are your ways my ways, declares the Lord.
For as the heavens are higher than the earth,
so are my ways higher than your ways
and my thoughts than your thoughts.

---

1. J. C. Ryle, *Holiness: Its Nature, Hindrances, Difficulties, and Roots* (London: James Clark & Co, 1956), p.154.

4. Despising God in Lust

After graduation Ed decided to spend a year serving a city church on an apprenticeship scheme. Ed grew strong in his faith and his passion for Christ as he spent his days in Bible studies, one-to-one discipleship and leading the youth work. When the year had finished Ed moved back in with his folks to look for a job in engineering, and he hoped to get stuck into his home church. Yet reconnecting with a couple of old school friends shifted his social life away from church. A quick pint on Friday night soon turned into wild partying and Ed stumbled into sexual sin; his drunken flings then unbolted his curiosity about porn, and within weeks his faith shattered into a mess of doubts and addiction. By the time Ed asked for help from his pastor he was actively questioning the inerrancy of the Bible and the resurrection of Christ. Yet he was so blinded by his lust that he didn't recognise that it was his love for sin that was calling his faith into question. Fortunately, Ed's pastor was able lovingly to challenge him and to support him out of his backsliding.

Blinded by Lust

King David was another believer blinded by his lust. One day he was worshipping in the street 'with all his might' (2 Sam. 6:14) yet four chapters later he steals a man's wife straight from her bathtub, and murders the husband to cover it up (2 Sam. 11). How did he fall so quickly? Did it not occur to David when he was gawping at Bathsheba that he was not keeping covenant with his eyes? Or that he was throwing himself in front of the lust bus by sending for her? His covenant God was obviously not on his mind when he was alone with her. David was so driven by his lust he had no thought of God at all.

David's first mistake was dropping his guard; picking the easy ride, lazily lounging around his palace penthouse instead of going out to war with his own army (2 Sam. 11:1-2). This led to David's sexual passion killing his passion for God. David's lust left him so blind that when the prophet Nathan challenged his behaviour through an analogy, he self-righteously demanded death for his own merciless crime (2 Sam. 12:5, 7). He was the thieving rich man who killed a poor man's treasured lamb.

The Power of ~~Love~~ Lust

David's sexual appetite didn't just *eclipse* his appetite for God; it temporarily *killed* it. David, this man so passionate for his covenant God, actively hated and loathed God in his adultery. The Lord says through Nathan His prophet: 'you have despised me and have taken the wife of Uriah the Hittite to be your wife' (2 Sam. 12:10). It is a helpful reminder to us that the text doesn't read, 'you despised me when you took the wife of Uriah'. We turn our backs on

God well before we sin physically; David did it when he was ogling at Bathsheba, when he asked who she was, and when he used his authority to take what was not his.

Digital Davids

Unfortunately, we don't need the height of a palace roof to engage in explicit eyeballing; it is readily available to us in our pockets, on our screens, in books and magazines. Our lustful planning, our sluggish accountability, idly avoiding setting up account security, logging on, unrestrained tapping from link to link hungry for digital sex. This sin is as shameless and as destructive as David's. In all our sexual impurity we hate the beauty of Christ and stupidly love the ugliness of sin.

So Destructive

Have you cooled in your faith and backslidden because of sexual sin? Or perhaps you are lukewarm because you are guilt-ridden from past sexual sin? Lust eats Christians up for dinner and then spits them out broken and bleeding. We've all seen it. Every church youth group has teenagers who have forsaken their passion for Christ for physical freedom with their boyfriends or girlfriends. Many of us have friends who are spiritually stunted in their addiction to porn, stuck in a circle of desire and remorse. Or we've painfully watched beloved church leaders walk out on their churches because they can no longer fight their same-sex attraction or the opportunity for adultery. Lust is so destructive and it is the sure road to spiritual difficulty.

Fight Lust with Christ

Sexual sin was rife amongst the Christians in Corinth. So, Paul challenges them with the words: 'The body is not meant for sexual immorality, but for the Lord, and the Lord for the body' (1 Cor. 6:13). God didn't *make* our bodies for sexual sin and He certainly didn't *save* them for it. Our mouths, hands, heads, skin, and sexual organs are all meant for the Lord Jesus Christ and He is meant for them. This is because as Christians we are united to Christ. 'Do you not know that your bodies are members of Christ?' (1 Cor. 6:15). This spiritual oneness with King Jesus is powerful and impacts our physical bodies. Using our skin-covered temples of the Holy Spirit to sin against God, to despise Him, is seriously damaging.

If you are spiritually backsliding because of lust and sexual sin then call upon the Lord and reassign your sexual hankering to a hankering for the goodness and beauty of Christ. Sexual sin is hard to fight but we can fight it with Christ. Christ is better. Think of Samwise Gamgee in Tolkien's *The Return of the King*:

> *The Ring tempted him, gnawing at his will and reason. Wild fantasies arose in his mind; and he saw Samwise the Strong, Hero of the Age, striding with a flaming sword across the darkened land, and armies flocking to his call as he marched to the overthrow of Barad-dûr. He had only to put on the Ring and claim it for his own, and all this could be. In that hour of trial it was the love of his master that helped most to hold him firm.*[1]

---

1. J. R. R. Tolkien, *The Return of the King* (London: HarperCollins Publishers, 2001) p. 206.

It is love for our Master, King Jesus, that is our motivation to resist and stand firm in the hour of temptation. I write this on Maundy Thursday, the day we focus on Jesus, the innocent God-man struggling in a garden with blood and sweat to take on a hideous death He did not deserve, for our rebellion, fancies, whims and addictions. For the Christian devoted to Christ, mindless indulgence lies too close to home. Remember! You are united to your Saviour who had nails hammered through His hands for when you can't control your own.

No 'beyond grace'

'But you don't know how sinful I've been! I'm beyond grace!' There is no 'beyond grace' with Jesus Christ. Like Him, His grace is supernatural. Christ's death at Calvary was bigger than our human sin and in His death, His grace is sufficient for all of us (2 Cor. 12:9). When we think our sin is too big for Christ we are struggling with unbelief and we need the person of the Holy Spirit to work in us. Returning to God from backsliding is basking in a gospel that is not about us or how big our sin is, but how big God's grace is in Christ Jesus.

PRAYER:

Father God, Help me to believe that you can forgive my sexual impurity and unfaithfulness. May your Spirit teach me the power of the blood of your Holy Son Jesus Christ and that your grace is sufficient even for me.

In Jesus' name,

Amen.

5. Job's Naked Worship

We have seen that pleasure and comfort can pull us away from God, but so can pain. In the bitter seasons of life, people wander away from God because they feel He has let them down. Most, however, struggle on and experience a numbing distance towards the Lord. Here we are dealing with the searing pain, failures, and disappointments of life that can distract and dull our love for Christ.

Have you been journeying through a time of spiritual darkness? Are you caught in the pitiless waves of grief? Or burnt out with anxiety about your family, money, health, or ministry? Maybe these things have wasted away your enjoyment of Jesus. You still believe but the gospel feels disconnected. You are a believer and you know you are alive in Christ, but you feel spiritually suffocated by disappointment and sorrow.

I Can't Pray

As we will see, suffering doesn't have to shift our eyes away from the Lord. Of course, life can really challenge and test our faith. At these times, we are desperate for God's comfort but feel abandoned in our grief, plagued with questions that God fails to answer. One Christian family who lost their healthy toddler in his sleep begged for prayer because their grief and shock had left them spiritually mute; they could not pray. Job too, and many of us, have been stunned by God's painful providences. In the book of Job we find a man very honestly wrestling with God, yet staying faithful in suffering. Job's wife, however, stands in contrast to her husband. She allows her grief to turn into an anger that pulls her into a spiritually desolate place. Her anger is her pitfall and she does not fight for worship.

Naked Worship

Job was a godly man with family (ten children), money (a lot of camels), and power (lots of servants) (Job 1:1-3). He had it all ... Until he lost it all in one tragic afternoon. Then, when all he has left is his health, he loses that too, reduced to a shadow of a man sitting in black ashes. Job is as broken as the pot he uses to scrape his blistering skin (*cf.* 2:8). And what does he do? He worships.

> *Then Job arose and tore his robe and shaved his head and fell on the ground and worshipped. And he said, 'Naked I came from my mother's womb, and naked shall I return. The LORD gave, and the LORD has taken away; blessed be the name of the LORD.'* (Job 1:20-21)

It's easy to gloss over the tragedy of Job's situation and just think of him as a Bill Gates reduced to a smelly, nauseating beggar. But think about his grief in relation to yours. Job is completely heartbroken. All of his babies are dead, all his possessions have been ripped from his hands, he has no physical relief, no bed, no medicines, and no comfort in his wife (*cf.* 2:9, 19:14). He says he is naked because he has nothing; everything has been stripped away. But Job still worships. The pain is endless and he wants to die (7:3).

Yet he does not backslide.

He does not sin.

He fights for worship.

Faithful

We can sometimes misunderstand the author of Job and think that Job was perfect; but he wasn't. He was a sinner like you and me. Otherwise God would not have needed to challenge him in chapters 38 to 41. But as a man passionate for God's glory (Job 1:5), Job keeps himself above reproach. Through these painful providences he is faithful. God knew Job would maintain his spiritual integrity, that's why God did not stop Satan's hand (Job 2:6). And so, James uses him as a model of faithfulness in suffering.

> *As an example of suffering and patience, brothers, take the prophets who spoke in the name of the Lord. Behold, we consider those blessed who remained steadfast. You have heard of the steadfastness of Job, and you have seen the purpose of the Lord, how the Lord is compassionate and merciful.* (James 5:10-11)

God has Gone

But Job's steadfastness doesn't minimise the spiritual strain and distress he is in. Job recalls his walk with God when all was well. 'I was in my prime, when the friendship of

God was upon my tent, when the Almighty was yet with me, when my children were all around me' (Job 29:4-5). How we also pine for past seasons of joy, safety, and content, when we are in the spiritual and emotional darkness of loss. And like us, Job too attempts to articulate his pain and make sense of it. 'And now my soul is poured out within me; days of affliction have taken hold of me' (Job 30:16). Job continues saying that God 'multiplies my wounds without cause' (Job 9:17); 'Why do you hide your face and count me as your enemy?' (Job 13:24).

Many of us know some of Job's trials: when the cancer or the car accident that only happens to other people is now in our own skin and bones. Or when we are attacked by our church family and inflicted with deep wounds. Suffering tests our faith, we can feel far from God, and it is difficult to worship.

Suffering and Satan

In part, we backslide in suffering because we don't resist Satan. Peter warns us: 'Be sober-minded; be watchful. Your adversary the devil prowls around like a roaring lion, seeking someone to devour' (1 Pet. 5:8). Satan wants to kill faith. Don't forget if Satan was writing this book it would be a 'how to' guide; he wants us to stumble and fall. He is probably quite content with lukewarm Christians. Satan triumphed in the life of Job's wife when she said to him 'curse God and die' (Job 2:9). Both Job and his wife knew God was responsible for their grief. But while Job weeps and worships, she curses God. She was happy to worship God when she had her family and wealth. She wanted God's *gifts*, not Him. She is like many of us; when all God's gifts are stripped away she backslides in unbelief and anger.

Suffering is Pointless

In the 1999 film *Notting Hill*, Bella, a character paralysed from falling down the stairs and struggling with infertility, offers her take on suffering. 'Don't take it personally. The more I think about things, the more I see no rhyme or reason in life. No one knows why some things work out and some things don't.' This is typical of the world's view of suffering: we sometimes have bad luck, it is arbitrary and meaningless. This means the world sees the damning diagnosis — relentless unemployment or miscarriage, the despair of dad leaving, the unsolvable nag of financial debt, the dark silence of depression, loneliness or infertility, and death stealing away someone we love — as completely pointless.

But there is no such thing as pointless suffering in the Bible.

The Biblical Theology of Suffering

As those who trust in a *good* and *sovereign* God, it is *impossible* for Christians to believe their suffering is pointless. Firstly, because of the cross. The suffering and death of the Lord Jesus at Calvary is the climax of God's work and purposes. There God ordained immense and undeserved suffering to bring about eternal redemption and glory. Christ's suffering is the lens through which we should see our own. Of course, our pain is not redemptive like His, but it also has eternal significance.

> *... But if when you do good and suffer for it you endure, this is a gracious thing in the sight of God. For to this you have been called, because Christ also suffered for you ... When he was reviled, he did not revile in return, ... but continued entrusting himself to him who judges justly. He himself bore our sins in his body on the tree ....* (1 Pet. 2:20-21, 23-24)

And secondly, because the Bible teaches us that our own trials test and work out our faith in the same way pulling weights builds up our muscles.

> *... you have been grieved by various trials, so that the tested genuineness of your faith — more precious than gold that perishes though it is tested by fire — may be found to result in praise and glory ....* (1 Pet. 1:6-7)

Like Job, we have to fight for faith, wielding a biblical theology of suffering when the pain and the darkness is unyielding, giving us deep gospel hope that keeps us blessing the name of the Lord.

THINK:

Are you excusing sin in your life because you are going through a tough time? What changes can you make?

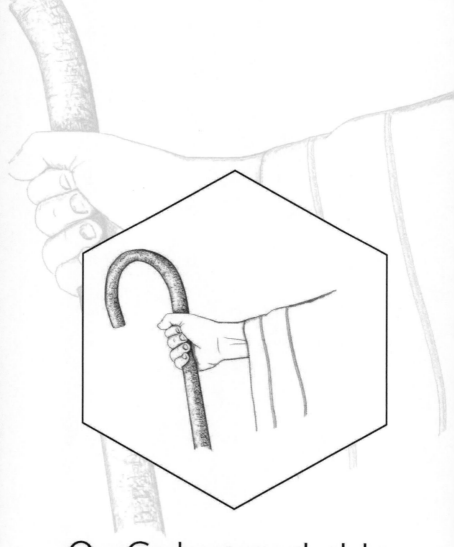

Our God restores the lukewarm and the backsliding
with tenderness

Part Two: Gospel Comfort

What we need when we are lukewarm and backsliding is mighty, meaty truths of the gospel to comfort our souls and re-fix our eyes on King Jesus.

6. Embracing Lukewarm Weakness

At the moment Hollywood is inundating us with super-hero films. It seems every few months a new superhero emerges with a different story of zero-to-hero, new super-powers, and a freshly ironed cloak. In the good old days, it was a martial arts flick: Bruce Lee or Mr Miyagi elegantly restoring justice to the world with lightning fast blocks and seamless round-house kicks. No CGI; just authentic Kung-fu.

But have you ever wondered why these fighting machines or superheroes are so cool ... why we like watching them? Or, if you are not into superheroes, why do we human beings find it exhilarating to watch films or programmes about high-flying entrepreneurs or fast cars? Why are these things so appealing to us?

Power. It's about the power. Feeling your own invincibility pulsing through your veins, the money to live literally on top of the world, to do whatever, whenever, or the roaring shift of 300 plus horsepower with a squeeze of your toes. There is a subtle desire for power in all of us. We crave it and get a thrill when Hollywood or the BBC dish out imaginary moments of it.

Glorious Weakness

But when we are struggling in our faith and broken over our sin, we have no power. We are weak and helpless, cut-up by our vile pride and the ugliness of our hearts, depressed by the spiritual darkness in which we find ourselves. We hate this brokenness and weakness because we want to be self-sufficient and in control; we want to feel power. But, of course, this place of weakness is a good place to be. These moments show us the truth of our spiritual condition. Perhaps you are now painfully aware of your rebellious, wandering heart, and feel sorrow for the sin inside you. You've lost your spiritual self-sufficiency and busyness. Embrace it! Being spiritually weak and broken is glorious because it makes us hungry for God.

Paul was weak before God and he embraced it ... he even boasted about it! 'I will boast all the more gladly of my weaknesses, so that the power of Christ may rest upon me' (2 Cor. 12:9). Don't get me wrong; Paul's weakness was presumably not lukewarm faith and no one should boast about their sin. Yet in light of his thorn in the flesh, Paul bragged about his weakness because the Lord had said to him: 'My grace is sufficient for you, for my power is made perfect in weakness' (2 Cor. 12:9). One radical and counter-cultural gospel comfort to the lukewarm and backsliding, is their own weakness and Christ's perfect strength.

Beggars before Christ

Jonah was a high-profile preacher who disobeyed God and got more than just stuck in a puddle of fish phlegm; death was so close he could taste it (Jonah 2:1-7). He became a perfect picture of spiritual weakness and helplessness. He couldn't buck up and break out. He couldn't enter his 'mind-palace' to outwit the fish or God. In Jonah chapter 2 we find him begging for God to hear him. He throws himself on God's grace because he knows without it he is lost forever.

We are all weak and in glorious need of Christ. For it was 'while we were still weak, at the right time Christ died for the ungodly' (Rom. 5:6). There is a legend that written on a scrap of paper, or from his lips, Martyn Luther's last words were:

We are beggars. This is true.

We are all beggars before Christ; prophets and preachers included. We are the leper who got on his knees and begged Jesus to heal him (Mark 1:40) and the woman who stealthily touched Jesus because she was desperate to be healed of her bleeding (Mark 5:25-34). Whether the gospel is new to us or we have preached it for decades is irrelevant. As Christians, we are those who have cried out with the blind man at the roadside of Jericho: 'Jesus, Son of David, have mercy on me!' (Luke 18:38).

If you are broken and desperate for God's grace to heal and strengthen you, then call on Him. Our God restores the lukewarm and the backsliding with tenderness. 'A bruised reed he will not break, and a smouldering wick he will not quench' (Matt. 12:20).

PRAY: Psalm 102:1-2

Hear my prayer, O LORD; let my cry come to you!
Do not hide your face from me
in the day of my distress!
Incline your ear to me;
answer me speedily in the day when I call!

7. The Shepherd's Joy

When I drive through Wales I think on the odds of the parable of the Lost Sheep. There are a lot of sheep in Wales, and when you think you have seen all the sheep there are to be seen, you realise you have only just got off the M4 and actually the sheep have only just got started.

So, one asks: when sheep are in such excellent supply, would a shepherd really leave 99% of his goods unwatched to go off to find one daft sheep that has wandered off? Would he really bother when he has so many? I mean it's just one sheep!

But we miss so easily the point of this parable. Sheep were a treasured commodity in Jesus' day. That's why they were given a shepherd. They weren't left to roam around unattended on roadsides like they are now. But were valued as significant to one's livelihood and status, and tended by a loyal caretaker. Back then, it was never 'just one sheep'!

It is the same for us. If we stray away from Christ, we are not left to our own devices, brushed aside as an insignificant fraction. We are never 'just one sheep'! Jesus told this parable because the Pharisees were criticising Him for spending time with sinners.

> *What man of you, having a hundred sheep, if he has lost one of them, does not leave the ninety-nine in the open country, and go after the one that is lost, until he finds it? And when he has found it, he lays it on his shoulders, rejoicing.* (Luke 15:4-5)

Jesus tells them He will always go out and hunt for His lost sheep. And when they are found, He is overjoyed, 'When he comes home, he calls together his friends and his neighbours, saying to them, "Rejoice with me, for I have found my sheep that was lost"' (Luke 15:6). Although like fickle sheep we may wander away and end up getting stuck on a steep mountainside or tangled up in barbed wire, Jesus Christ, with His endless grace and mercy, always hunts us down.

Doesn't God want me Back?

Many of us have experienced times when we feel abandoned by God and we find ourselves asking Him, 'Don't you want me back?' But King Jesus is the Good Shepherd. He is not a hired hand. He is deeply committed to His people and has bought us back from our backsliding with His own blood. Jesus endured the pain and horror of the cross for us so He isn't going to just let us go. He said:

> *I am the good shepherd. I know my own and my own know me, just as the Father knows me and I know the Father; and I lay down my life for the sheep.* (John 10:14-15)

After He tells the parable of the Lost Sheep, Jesus moves onto the parables of the Lost Coin and the Prodigal Son (Luke 15:8-32). Both stories make the same point: Jesus Christ finds lost things! And His grace pursues us both B.C. and A.D.; before we become a Christian and all the way through our lives.

God's Joy

It is important for us to notice that throughout these three parables in Luke 15 Jesus speaks of heaven's joy. With the sheep safely secured upon the shepherd's shoulders (there's a tongue-twister) He compares the joy of the shepherd with that of heaven when we repent: 'Just so, I tell you, there will be more joy in heaven over one sinner who repents than over ninety-nine righteous persons' (Luke 15:7). And again, after the coin is found: '"Rejoice with me, for I have found the coin that I had lost." Just so, I tell you, there is joy before the angels of God over one sinner who repents' (v. 9b-10). And in the story of the Prodigal Son, the father doesn't run, embrace, kiss, and throw a mean party because he is disappointed. Instead he says, 'it was fitting to celebrate and be glad, for this your brother was dead, and is alive; he was lost, and is found' (v. 32).

It is this joy that drove God to extend His saving arm to sinners; it is this joy that led Jesus Christ the Son of God to the cross. 'Looking to Jesus, the founder and perfecter of our faith, who *for the joy that was set before him* endured the cross, despising the shame, and is seated at the right hand of the throne of God' (Heb. 12:2, emphasis added).

Some of us talk about Christian Hedonism and our joy in God. But we can also revel and dance because our

57

salvation in Christ Jesus gives the mighty Godhead, and the angels, deep joy. And this is the case when we call upon Christ for the first time, the second time, or the twenty-third time.

MEDITATE:

When they had mocked him, they stripped him of the purple cloak and put his own clothes on him ... they crucified him and divided his garments among them (Mark 15:20, 24)

[John] turned and saw a man ... clothed with a long robe and with a golden sash round his chest. (Rev 1:12, 13)

... Twisting together a crown of thorns, they put it on him ... And they were striking his head with a reed and spitting on him (Mark 15:17, 19)

The hairs of his head were white, like white wool, like snow (Rev 1:14)

They also blindfolded him and kept asking him, 'Prophesy! Who is it that struck you?' (Luke 22:64)

... His eyes were like a flame of fire (Rev 1:14)

When Jesus had received the sour wine, he said, 'It is finished,' and he bowed his head and gave up his spirit. (John 19:30)

...his voice was like the roar of many waters. In his right hand he held seven stars, from his mouth came a sharp two-edged sword, and his face was like the sun shining in full strength ... he laid his right hand on me, saying, ... 'I am the first and the last, and the living one. I died, and behold I am alive for evermore' (Rev. 1:15-18).

8. I Can't Pray

Simon left the tube station and walked into a city scene that resembled the dreary watercolour nailed to his parents' landing wall. Falling into step with the same body of commuters he nudged and bumped every morning, Simon's heart sank as he remembered the church prayer meeting was scheduled for that evening. He felt a stab of regret that he felt so distant from God.

When I remember God, I moan; when I meditate, my spirit faints. (Ps. 77:3)

He turned a corner and crossed the road. 'What can I do?' he asked himself, wedging himself onto the crammed pedestrian island. 'When I prayed last night I really thought God would answer me. But then it all felt so half-hearted … and I don't even know if He heard me,' he thought.

I cry aloud to God, aloud to God, and he will hear me. (Ps. 77:1)

Simon crossed the road and pushed the door to his office building, trying to lid the frustration welling up inside.

In the day of my trouble I seek the Lord; in the night my hand is stretched out without wearying; my soul refuses to be comforted. (Ps. 77:2)

Holy Groans

Prayer remains the hardest part of the Christian life. Even when we are really enjoying God many of us find it tricky. So, if we are spiritually dry or flat it can be near impossible. This isn't surprising if prayer is the chief muscle of faith. When our faith is lukewarm, our prayer muscle goes saggy and we forget how to pray. We want God but are tongue-tied. Also, there are the times when life devastates us and in our grief and sorrow we have no words. Then we can do nothing but groan. And God hears our groans.

The letter of Romans tells us that when we can't pray we have an intercessor.

Likewise the Spirit helps us in our weakness. For we do not know what to pray for as we ought, but the Spirit himself intercedes for us with groanings too deep for words. (Rom. 8:26)

How encouraging that the Holy Spirit prays with holy groans on our behalf. When we are wrestling in spiritual darkness or profound loss, our greatest comfort is the Comforter Himself; the Holy Spirit who dwells with us and in us (John 14:17). His presence is one of the greatest comforts in being a Christian, and His help is given to *all* who belong to Christ (Rom. 8:9).

Not Voiceless Orphans

The Holy Spirit groans for us in prayer because we are adopted; we have joined God's covenant family.

> *For all who are led by the Spirit of God are sons of God ...* [and] *have received the Spirit of adoption as sons, by whom we cry, 'Abba! Father!'* (Rom. 8:14-15)

This is why when Jesus promises the Holy Spirit He says 'I will not leave you as orphans' (John 14:18). We are not voiceless orphans who stick out a hand on a street corner, begging for money or scraps of food. We are children of God and co-heirs with Christ (Rom. 8:16-17).

This means that when we can't pray, when sin or pain leaves us hoarse, confused and undeserving, we don't need to be timid orphans, like Oliver Twist requesting some more. We are adopted children of God and co-heirs with the King, even when we don't feel like it. We can call out to God and He hears us as His treasured children.

PRAY:
Abba! Father!
May your Holy Spirit show me that I am not an orphan but adopted into your family. Teach me how to pray and show me how to take hold of Christ.
In Jesus' name I pray,
Amen.

---

9. Hunted to the Cross

Are you taunted and haunted by your sin? Have you spent years or decades chewing remorsefully on your past; replaying mistakes and regrets when you can't sleep? As believers, we tell ourselves that we are forgiven and it has been dealt with by Christ. But we don't believe it. We continue to harbour guilt, and these memories, some horrid, some embarrassing, some traumatic, harass our spiritual lives and hamper our joy in Christ.

Finished

On the cross, Jesus Christ said 'It is finished!' (John 19:30). Finished! Christ's death was the end. The death of our sin and guilt. If we belong to Jesus then there is no sin unforgiven left to taunt us. Why should we hang our heads in shame when He hung *naked* on a tree? If you are a Christian, you are free! This is the good news: God in Christ has cast *all* your sin into the depths of the sea (Micah 7:19) and there is '*no* condemnation for those who are in Christ Jesus' (Rom. 8:1). You cannot condemn yourself anymore, Jesus bore it on the cross.

We said earlier that the only reason Christians wander away from God is because of sin. But Jesus Christ has died for our lukewarmness, our apathy, or our backsliding; past, present and future. It is gone! It is finished because the perfect spotless lamb was led silently to the slaughter for the wandering sheep (Isa. 53:7).

Crucified with Christ

I think we find it hard to believe that Jesus, at the cross, has actually rid us of our sin. For how can a 2,000-year-old Roman cross save you and me now in the twenty-first century? We were not at Golgotha that day on Passover week.

Praise God, Calvary is not suspended in time, irrelevant to us without Doctor Who's Tardis or a quantum leap! It is by the Christian's union with Christ, forged by the Holy Spirit, that His death becomes our death and His resurrection victory becomes our resurrection victory. We are saved by faith in Christ because we are 'crucified *with* Christ'. As Paul wrote 'it is no longer I who live, but Christ who lives in me' (Gal. 2:20).

Defogging the Cross

There are times in the Christian life when the cross is bright and as clear as day to us. We get it. We revel in it. But in spiritual drought and temptation, the cross becomes murky and the gospel can seem almost mythical and detached from our everyday lives.

Taking a long hard look at the cross of Christ can clear the fog. When we 'set' the dying Lord of lords and King of kings before us, our 'heart is glad, and [our] whole being rejoices' (Ps. 16:8-9). It is a huge comfort that the cross of Christ cannot change. It's finished! And this historical event doesn't shift depending on how spiritual we feel or the success of our ministry.

Let Christ hunt you back to the cross and show you that your sin is 'as far as the east is from the west' (Ps. 103:12).

SING:

'Tis finished! The Messiah dies,
Cut off for sin, but not his own.
Accomplished is the sacrifice,
The great redeeming work is done.

The veil is rent; in Christ alone
The living way to heaven is seen;
The middle wall is broken down,
And all the world may enter in.

'Tis finished! All my guilt and pain,
I want no sacrifice beside;
For me, for me the Lamb is slain;
'Tis finished! I am justified.

The reign of sin and death is o'er,
And all may live from sin set free;
Satan hath lost his mortal power;
'Tis swallowed up in victory.

(Charles Wesley, 1762)

---

10. I'm Not Dead!

Bones. Bones everywhere. Dry. Cracked. Lifeless. White and naked. No tissue. No red life-giving blood. Good for nothing. Just empty skulls, filling the valley like sweets in a jar, and bones piled high like sticks.

Can these bones live?

Helen sat sipping her mochaccino, her eyes were downcast but she seemed restless.

'What's up, Helen?' Caroline asked as she sat down opposite her. 'You're obviously not yourself.'

Helen looked at her friend and smiled weakly, relieved she was getting to the point. 'I'm really struggling at the moment ... spiritually, I mean. Have for a few months. I feel so ... well ... flat. I don't know what to do.'

'Oh, Helen! I'm sorry ... Are you able to pray about it?'

Helen put her coffee down and shook her head. 'Not really. I don't seem to be able to pray at all!' She locked her eyes on her friend and frowned. 'I feel so closed off from the things of God. I feel numb … dead! Like someone has taken a pair of secateurs to my spiritual nervous system.'

Dead or Alive?

Agreed, the Christian life isn't all about feelings and some might say that they have been referred to too many times in this book. But the Christian life is an experience; it is something to be known *and* felt.[1] When we are shrouded in grief, or fighting against our own apathy or rebellion, our emotions are overwhelming. In moments of spiritual difficulty, many believers have known a sense of desertion from God, and feel spiritually numb or dead inside.

Whenever we feel this way, however, there are only two possibilities. Simply that we *are* spiritually dead and need to make Christ Jesus our Saviour. Or that we are *not* dead, but a Christian; united and alive with Jesus Christ. Whether we feel it or not. For 'God, being rich in mercy, because of the great love with which he loved us, even when we were dead in our trespasses, made us alive together with Christ — by grace you have been saved' (Eph. 2:4-5).

Can These Bones Live?

> … *There was a sound, and behold, a rattling, and the bones came together, bone to its bone. And I looked, and behold, there were sinews on them, and flesh had come upon them, and skin had covered them. But there was no breath in them … and the breath came into them, and they lived and stood on their feet …*. (Ezek. 37:7-8, 10)

1. Stuart Olyott, *Something Should be Known and Felt* (Bridgend: Bryntirion Press, 2014).

Through the death and resurrection of His Son, God gives spiritual life to those who are dead. He does this by the power of the Spirit of Christ, turning hearts of stone into hearts of flesh (Ezek. 3:26). If you have made Jesus your Lord and Saviour then you are alive! Alive because you are fused to Christ by the power of the Holy Spirit. Hallelujah!

Ultimate Victory

A couple of Februarys ago, my husband and I buried one of our babies. We could make no sense of our loss. The pain only hewed at our insides.

With our miscarriage came a deluge of physical and emotional mess. First death was inside me, and then we had to bury our dear sweet baby in the cold, hard ground. I can tell you our theology was tested and maxed out as we poured all our sorrow and hope into the coming of Easter: the mighty victory of Jesus Christ over death. Our comfort was, and is still found, in the fact that we revel in union with Him who is 'the resurrection and the life' (John 11:25).

The victory of Jesus stamping out sin and death is our victory in bereavement and loss, as well as in times of cold faith and apathy; for we *are* alive because He *is* alive! The victory of Jesus Christ coming out of the grave is also our triumph in temptation, our healing in backsliding, and our joy in apathy. When we stare death in the face or when we are frustrated and numb, sin and death and hell have been defeated. When the darkness persists all we can do is preach to ourselves that we are spiritually alive and kicking by the Holy Spirit until it rolls away. Our hope is that 'if we have been united with him in a death like his, we shall certainly be united with him in a resurrection like his' (Rom. 6:5).

READ: Matthew 28: 1-10

Now after the Sabbath, toward the dawn of the first day of the week, Mary Magdalene and the other Mary went to see the tomb. And behold, there was a great earthquake, for an angel of the Lord descended from heaven and came and rolled back the stone and sat on it. His appearance was like lightning, and his clothing white as snow. And for fear of him the guards trembled and became like dead men. But the angel said to the women, 'Do not be afraid, for I know that you seek Jesus who was crucified. He is not here, for he has risen, as he said. Come, see the place where he lay. Then go quickly and tell his disciples that he has risen from the dead, and behold, he is going before you to Galilee; there you will see him. See, I have told you.' So they departed quickly from the tomb with fear and great joy, and ran to tell his disciples. And behold, Jesus met them and said, 'Greetings!' And they came up and took hold of his feet and worshiped him. Then Jesus said to them, 'Do not be afraid; go and tell my brothers to go to Galilee, and there they will see me.'

Take hold of Jesus and move into a place of obedience, safety and unshakeable joy

Part Three: Practical Self-Care

Now we are going to consider some safeguards to keep us from becoming lukewarm.

11. Physical and Spiritual Burnout

We have covered a lot of ground in our short time together; giving gospel comfort to those straying, as well as exploring why we wander from God at all. We know the main problem is sin, and the fact that we live in a fallen world. Our desire for material comfort (Demas and Lot), our carnal passions (David), or our fear (Jonah) are some pitfalls that trip us up from enjoying Jesus. Still, the reasons behind spiritual struggles are complex and personal to each of us.

Sometimes, however, we just burnout. Like Job, we are beaten down by the pressures of life. The consequences of existing in a fallen world pile up and then come crashing down on us. Frequently, something happens that is the last straw; the final weight that sends everything flying. We are all different: it might be the strain of family, work, debt or ill health. It might be criticism from a colleague or a house move. For Christian workers, it can be the endless plodding on in a discouraging ministry. Either way, frequently there is a trigger and suddenly we have nothing else to give; we are physically, mentally, spiritually and emotionally exhausted. In this spiritual exhaustion, if we allow our spiritual disciplines to slide, apathy certainly follows. And since we have little spiritual strength to fall upon, we may enter a time of serious spiritual struggle.

This is not the book to look at these things in detail. But we must explore briefly the relationship between a lukewarm life and physical and spiritual burnout.

Burnt-out

Chris is in his early forties. For years he balanced a demanding office life with a young family. But just as his company went through a busy merge and overhaul, Chris learnt his mother was showing signs of dementia. Things got complicated. Awkward phone calls with his father progressed, in a matter of days, into a refusal to care for her. All these triggers pressed Chris into a place of depression and stress. He lost his desire to pray and read Scripture, and felt detached from church life. What was Chris's sin? Was he at fault, or just living in a fallen world, groaning with sin?

Like Chris, are you spiritually dry because of the onslaught of life? Have you experienced the devastation of bereavement, infertility, depression or the loss of a marriage? Are you facing the disappointment of unwanted singleness, redundancy, disability or chronic ill health? If you are, like Chris, you need the gospel more than anything. But you probably need some self-care too.

We do, however, have to be honest with ourselves. We need to check we are not blaming our sin on something else.

Someone Else's Sin

It is important to flag up another complexity regarding sin and backsliding, that is, those who suffer not because of their sin but because of someone else's. The betrayal of abuse, adultery or family breakdown leaves the innocent party with long-term, life-changing hardships that they neither asked for nor deserved. Unfortunately, these can drain the Christian, hardening them, whilst softening their church commitment or biblical worldview.

Elizabeth is an example of this. As a committed Christian, she had been happily married to Doug for years. But when Elizabeth found out Douglas was emotionally involved with another woman, their marriage ended. Elizabeth was left with the humiliation of having to explain Douglas's betrayal to their Christian friends. This, together with parenting a wayward daughter alone, a painful financial settlement, and attending yet another anniversary celebration by herself, soon made Elizabeth hard and bitter. It wasn't long before her faith crumpled under her anger and resentment.

Although Chris and Elizabeth's circumstances are very different, more than anything they *both* need God's strengthening and healing. And time and space to reset themselves physically and emotionally.

Physical & Spiritual

It is said that whenever one of Martyn Lloyd-Jones's congregation came to him, expressing a time of spiritual depression, he would send them home with the prescription of some good hearty food and rest; self-care at a very basic level. If, after a week there was no improvement, they should return; but they rarely did. As a GP as well as a pastor, Lloyd-Jones appreciated that our physical and spiritual wellbeing are very much connected.

Physical tiredness leads to spiritual burnout. If you are prone to burnout, don't be super-spiritual; guard your rest and time off. You are human — you need rest! When burnout or depression threaten we should respond to the signs and take time out as soon as possible, for at least forty eight hours. This will help clear our head. We live on a busy and broken planet; full of sin and weakness. This is why God ordained a day of rest. With our worldview of human fallibility, Christians should be the first to advocate rest and sleep, and to respond to our own burnout or depression (as well as that of others) with grace and courage to seek pastoral support from godly Christian friends.

WRITE:
Jot down some ideas you can put in place to prevent you from burning out.

---

12. The Best Preacher in Town

Preaching to yourself is a cunning strategy to a life of enjoying Christ. Martyn Lloyd-Jones famously wrote in his book *Spiritual Depression: Its Causes and Cures*, 'Have you realised that most of your unhappiness in life is due to the fact that you are listening to yourself instead of talking to yourself? ... The main art in the matter of spiritual living is to know how to handle yourself. You have to take yourself in hand, you have to address yourself, preach to yourself.'[1]

Preaching gospel truth to myself has been revolutionary to my spiritual life. After all, we are constantly listening to ourselves and are very easily persuaded by the voice in our heads. At the end of the day this means the best preacher in town is you. Instead of listening to your depressing, self-pitying, and self-indulgent self, preach gospel glories to yourself. Though this can take some training, it means stopping yourself in your tracks in the face of temptation,

---

1. Dr Martyn Lloyd-Jones, *Spiritual Depression: Its Causes and Cures* (Grand Rapids: Eerdmans, 1965). pp.20-21.

or halting in the midst of a mundane day and leading yourself to worship and praise.

Oi, Soul!

Psalms 42 and 43 are biblical examples of taking oneself in hand. The Psalmist questions his own soul: 'Why are you cast down, O my soul, and why are you in turmoil within me? Hope in God; for I shall again praise him, my salvation and my God' (Ps. 42:5, 11; 43:5). Oi, soul! You don't want that! Look to God, He is your hope and your joy. He has saved you and set you free. Enjoy God, O my soul!

Preaching to ourselves is so basic and so obvious, but we miss it completely. For example, throughout the week we need to copy the biology of flies: after consuming our Sunday meal at church, bring it back up later. Regurgitating and chewing upon the sermons we hear is one secret of consistently enjoying Christ throughout the week.

Memorise

We can be fooled into thinking that Bible memorisation belongs to vintage Sunday-school with its prize boards, frumpy Sunday school teachers and rows of snotty kids with dodgy hair-cuts and shiny knees. Yet this mental hoarding of Scripture is setting up a God-breathed arsenal to fire upon self, sin and Satan. It is what the Psalmist does: 'I have stored up your word in my heart, that I might not sin against you' (Ps. 119:11). It is what Paul does in taking 'every thought captive to obey Christ' (2 Cor. 10:5).

We need to know God's Word in order to preach and apply it on demand, so take time to memorise Scripture and understand the biblical truths it is teaching. This is particularly important for those with a busy home life, for example those in the often spiritually barren years of parenting small children. The physical, emotional and mental toil leaves us exhausted before the evening has begun. And the morning leaves little opportunity for devotions because the day starts abruptly with a scream, an ominous commotion or a little person climbing into bed with you. I can't recommend Bible memorisation to you enough. As I muster myself for a day of servitude and diplomatic solutions in a few seconds, I have found praying out memorised verses an essential start to the day.

Also, for those of us spending our day amongst non-Christians — in the temptation and negative conversation, at times of unsavoury humour or disparagement, and when we are misunderstood for being a Christian — reciting a verse from God's Word will fortify our biblical principles and bring glory to God at that moment.

Whatever we do, we all exist to glorify God and enjoy Him. Preaching Scripture to ourselves is an important way to live this in the small things and the big things.

Looking Back

When we are lukewarm we question whether God is really with us — whether He has *ever* really been with us. In the Old Testament we see the Israelites constantly remembering the Exodus, the time when God led them out of Egypt and they passed through the waters of the Red Sea (Exod. 13-15). Even centuries later they continue to preach to themselves God's covenant goodness and salvation. In the same way, preaching to ourselves God's past faithfulness in our lives invigorates our faith. 'Return, O my soul, to your rest; for the LORD has dealt bountifully with you' (Ps. 116:7).

In Psalm 77 we see a believer struggling in his faith. He shares his distress; feeling spurned and forgotten by God (vv. 7-8), lifting his hands to God in the night, but with little comfort (v. 2). But he is not duped by his mood or difficulty. He knows how to handle himself and looks back to God's historical salvation.

> *Then I said, 'I will appeal to this,*
> *to the years of the right hand of the Most High.'*
> *I will remember the deeds of the* LORD;
> *yes, I will remember your wonders of old.*
> *I will ponder all your work,*
> *and meditate on your mighty deeds.* (Ps. 77:10-12)

And his mind lingers on God's rescue all those years ago at the Red Sea. 'When the waters saw you, O God, when the waters saw you, they were afraid ... Your way was through the sea, your path through the great waters ... You led your people like a flock by the hand of Moses and Aaron' (vv. 16, 19-20).

When doubts and anxiety strike, preach to yourself the years of the Most High. Recall the Lord's power and faithfulness to you throughout your life, and preach the wonderful and mighty cross of Christ to your soul.

QUESTION:

The Lord's Supper is an important way we remember and appeal to the cross of Christ as a church family. When we are lukewarm we need to feed spiritually on Christ and remember in this way. How can this change the way you take communion?

13. Godly Crampons

Straying from the Lord is scary stuff. Suddenly everything we knew and treasured seems alien and confusing; prayer feels like the first sign of madness and our beloved Bibles seem like gobbledegook. Sermons don't thrill us anymore and we just walk out of church feeling battered. Because we don't want to be judged and misunderstood, we don't share our struggles.

'I can't tell anyone ...'
'I'm a church deacon ...'
'I'm on the C.U. Exec ...'
'I'm the pastor!'

We stop talking to God because it is hard to avoid the subject with Him. And we stop talking to our brothers and sisters in Christ because we feel hypocritical. This means many of us become isolated and depressed. We may start to favour the company of non-Christians and if we are not careful 'lukewarm' moves quickly into something more serious.

Spikey Friends

You may be a Christian who is deeply committed to Christ but who gets distracted easily. Or you may be pretty constant and steadfast in your walk with God. Either way, we all need godly crampons. Crampons are footwear attachments with metal spikes that claw into ice or snow to give climbers and walkers a strong foothold; without them their feet would be slipping and dancing all over the place. Godly crampons are the strong, sharp friends who see our weaknesses and give honest, loving and firm support. They are the people who pray for us, who will challenge us about skipping church, our lack of prayerfulness, or thoughtless decisions.

When we love someone, we want to honestly challenge them when we see them heading for danger. We too should humbly accept the same from a godly crampon. 'Better is open rebuke than hidden love. Faithful are the wounds of a friend; profuse are the kisses of an enemy' (Prov. 27:5-6). Godly crampons can stop us from backsliding because we can call for help as soon as we start losing control, and they can lead us back to Christ with the power of prayer and God's Word. So, if a spikey friend challenges you, don't get defensive and back away from their friendship — they might just be your best friend at this time of lukewarmness.

If we are hungry for the world, then like Lot, we will gravitate towards those who loiter and linger in it. I am not saying that believers shouldn't have non-Christian friends; sadly, too many of us don't need to turn our phones off on Sunday mornings because all our friends are in church.

But we all need to be wise and humble to see when certain company is doing us no good because it is 'godless' and 'barren' (Job 15:34; cf. Ps. 1:1).

Confession

I encourage you to speak to a friend or your pastor. When I was stuck in spiritual apathy I spoke openly to a pastor friend of ours and this was one of my first steps to recovery. Because our friend is a godly crampon I wasn't judged but prayed for and loved, and facing up to my hard heart was liberating. This is not surprising considering God's encouragement to confess. 'Therefore, confess your sins to one another and pray for one another, that you may be healed' (James 5:16). 'If we confess our sins, he is faithful and just to forgive us our sins and to cleanse us from all unrighteousness' (1 John 1:9).

Malnourished in Marriage

What about Christians who are married to an unbeliever? Or those who are married to a Christian but their spouse does not share their spiritual hunger? Many Christians become spiritually malnourished because of the disinterest of their partner; they feel pulled in two. Frequently the more spiritually mature believer will unconsciously neglect their walk with the Lord because being close to God only makes this spiritual imbalance bigger and more painful. This is compounded when the husband is not the spiritual leader in the home, which is pretty common in today's church. Here spikey, godly friends can really spur us, challenging and encouraging us to grow in grace when we are divided at home.

There is not much more to say about godly crampons. But when looking for them, find the godliest ones you can find … and you can never have enough!

SHARE:
Make contact with a spikey, godly friend.

---

14. Fear and Trembling

I am a Christian of vague, callous and cowardly repentance. Too many times I have fought against my guilt with 'I-know-I-am-saved-so-sorry-and-let's-not-talk-about-it-anymore'. I don't look at my sin enough to hate it. I am apathetic about God's holiness and His vision for mine.

Many of us don't take repentance seriously because we don't take sin seriously. The horror of our sin matches the horror of the cross. The Lord Jesus was humiliated, lashed, tortured, cut, stabbed for our sin. On the cross, He became a bloody mess since '... without the shedding of blood there is no forgiveness of sins' (Heb. 9:22).

As contemporary Christians influenced by our society, we approach sin as victims, talking about 'sin in our lives' instead of 'our sin'; avoiding the hard truth that we are to blame, that we have stumbled. We push away our guilt instead of realising that it is a good, healthy and godly response to sin. I know that if I commit myself to a gutsy guilt[1] and thorough repentance, instead of a cowardly dismissal, I will hate sin more and know more victory against it. Sure, this takes prayer, tears and time but genuine repentance is the driving force of our quest for godliness. We can't strive for Christlikeness without it.

Saved for Holy

Part of this problem is due to the fact that we see our salvation in Christ separately from God's call to holiness. But we were saved so we could be holy. Paul writes, Christ 'chose us in him before the foundation of the world, that we should be holy and blameless before him' (Eph. 1:4). Peter agrees in his letter to the churches in Asia (*cf.* 1 Pet. 1:1-2). Our growing in godliness is not just a by-product of the gospel — it is the reason for the gospel.

Thorough Repentance

Like many of our news headlines, King David's sin against Bathsheba and Uriah was sordid and nauseating. One perversion led to another until he was guilty of some of the worst human crimes. But David was not cowardly in his repentance. In Psalm 51 we see him look his sin squarely in the face. He doesn't say much about his adultery, deception and murder in the Psalm because he looks at the roots of these sins, which are at the core of his being and have been there since the day he was conceived (v. 5). So, he focuses on his heart, pleading to his loving and faithful God to remove the filth.

---

1. A term used by John Piper (see www.desiringgod.org for sermons and articles).

Have mercy on me, O God,
  according to your steadfast love;
according to your abundant mercy
  blot out my transgressions.
Wash me thoroughly from my iniquity,
  and cleanse me from my sin! (Ps. 51:1-2).

David has guts enough to look at the evil in his heart because he knows God loves him, and he is confident that God *will* wash him and restore him.

Purge me with hyssop, and I shall be clean;
  wash me, and I shall be whiter than snow.
Let me hear joy and gladness;
  let the bones that you have broken rejoice. ...
Restore to me the joy of your salvation,
  and uphold me with a willing spirit. (Ps. 51:7-8, 12)

Healing after backsliding

God calls us to repentance because He loves us. After the Lord Jesus challenges the Laodiceans for being lukewarm in John's vision, He tells them He is rebuking them because He loves them. 'Those whom I love, I reprove and discipline, so be zealous and repent' (Rev. 3:19). This is good news. As those in Christ we repent in utter safety. It is not some risky exposure of ourselves to a capricious sovereign. When we are confessing our sins we may kneel in humility, but we do so standing in complete confidence of God's love, forgiveness and washing — just like David.

If you have wandered away from God into toxic sin that causes you pain and humiliating shame just to think about, revelling in God's steadfast love will heal you of this painful past. Guilt cannot fester in a spiritual life that literally jumps for joy because of God's redeeming love. Remember, when we turn to Christ, the sins we have committed are no longer found in the place where we committed them. We've already said, they are nailed onto a wooden cross stained with the blood of the God-man that gives forgiveness, eternal life and freedom.

How Do We Repent?

True biblical repentance is not complicated and secretive. It is simple. You are looking at your sin and asking God to forgive it and make you holy because of His Son Jesus Christ.

Scripture offers us invaluable blueprints for repentance. Check out Daniel 9:4-19, Micah 7:7-9, and Hosea 6:1-3, as well as the famous Psalm 51. When we use Scripture as our prayers of repentance, the Holy Spirit works powerfully through His Word, giving us sorrow for our sin.

To avoid being vague and cowardly, when we confess our sins it is helpful to name the areas in which you have stumbled, as well as asking the Spirit of Christ to reveal any unrecognised sin. And if repentance is looking at our hearts and meditating on the root of our errors, our holiness will benefit from some questioning. Why do I get stressed and cross? What were my motives in talking negatively about that person? Why did I respond in that way? I find pride to be the root of most of my sin. This means most of the time I am repenting for my pride and asking God to give me humility.

Some hugely holy, practical ideas are getting on our knees and, when we have wronged someone, actually going to them and asking for forgiveness — this seems completely out of the question for many of us. But repentance is radical stuff! If you find stamina in prayer is a problem, then try writing your prayer down. And give yourself time! Coming to God in this way means carving out time.

Active Faith

In his letter to the Philippians, Paul writes: 'Therefore, my beloved … work out your own salvation with fear and trembling' (Phil. 2:12). What does Paul mean by 'working out our salvation'? Aren't we saved by Jesus Christ? Isn't the gospel free grace? Yes, and yes! But this free grace gives the believer in Christ responsibility. Not a passive, vague and lazy faith but an active faith that works out and confirms this salvation; building ourselves up in our 'most holy faith and praying in the Holy Spirit, keep[ing ourselves] in the love of God' (Jude 20-21).

And this fear and trembling is that of the Philippian jailer, who woke up on shift to the prison doors hanging off their hinges. 'Trembling with fear he fell down before Paul and Silas. Then he brought them out and said, "Sirs, what must I do to be saved?"' (Acts 16:29-30). It is the response we should have to the gospel: awe of a holy God as we confront our sin.

Be encouraged! We can successfully press on in our salvation only because God is working too. Paul goes on: 'for it is God who works in you, both to will and to work for his good pleasure' (Phil. 2:13). Jude confirms the same: 'Now to him who is able to keep you from stumbling and to present you blameless before the presence of his glory

91

with great joy' (Jude 24). God's 'good pleasure' and 'great joy' is our confidence to live out our repentance in fear and trembling.

THINK:

As you think upon your own sin, meditate on these glorious words included in Psalm 51; BLOT, WASH, CLEANSE, PURGE, CLEAN, WHITER, RENEW, RESTORE, and JOY. Let them lead you to Calvary.

15. Am I Actually a Christian?

Perhaps you picked up this book because you have been lukewarm or backslidden for months or years. Let's look at a verse we started out with.

> For thus says the Lord GOD: Behold, I, I myself will search for my sheep and will seek them out ... I will seek the lost, and I will bring back the strayed, and I will bind up the injured, and I will strengthen the weak (Ezek. 34:11, 16)

The Lord God is hunting you out; in His grace He is on your heels. If you respond to Him then He will sling you around His shoulders and carry you to a place of rejoicing. His love and forgiveness will cover your pain and guilt. For *all* your sins have been covered by Jesus Christ; this includes your apathy and backsliding. Even if you are prone to wandering away from God, Jesus died for your straying — past, present and future — in the same way that he died for everything else! Turn your guilt and remorse to repentance. Take hold of Jesus and move into a place of obedience, safety and unshakeable joy.

I don't know *when* I became a Christian, I only know I *am* a Christian. If you are questioning whether you belong to Jesus, it is important not to get distracted with these questions, 'am I actually a Christian?' 'when did I become a Christian?' Just make sure you are a Christian now! If you were trapped in a burning building, you would not spend time thinking about which floor you are managing to escape from, or what time of day it is. You would just make sure you are out; safe from the deadly smoke and flames! It is the same with the gospel. Just make sure you are united to Jesus; put your faith in Him and in His work for you at the cross, and be forgiven. Call on Him and He will deliver you 'from the domain of darkness' and transfer you 'to the kingdom of his beloved Son, in whom we have redemption, the forgiveness of sins' (Col. 1:13-14).

SHARE:

Speak with your pastor or a church leader and they will pray with you and give personal and biblical counsel.

Christian Focus Publications

Our mission statement —

STAYING FAITHFUL

In dependence upon God we seek to impact the world through literature faithful to His infallible Word, the Bible. Our aim is to ensure that the Lord Jesus Christ is presented as the only hope to obtain forgiveness of sin, live a useful life and look forward to heaven with Him.

Our books are published in four imprints:

CHRISTIAN
FOCUS

Popular works including biographies, commentaries, basic doctrine and Christian living.

CHRISTIAN
HERITAGE

Books representing some of the best material from the rich heritage of the church.

MENTOR

Books written at a level suitable for Bible College and seminary students, pastors, and other serious readers. The imprint includes commentaries, doctrinal studies, examination of current issues and church history.

CF4•K

Children's books for quality Bible teaching and for all age groups: Sunday school curriculum, puzzle and activity books; personal and family devotional titles, biographies and inspirational stories — because you are never too young to know Jesus!

Christian Focus Publications Ltd,
Geanies House, Fearn, Ross-shire,
IV20 1TW, Scotland, United Kingdom.
www.christianfocus.com
blog.christianfocus.com